Ijapa's Fun with the Alphabet

English Hausa Igbo Yoruba

multilingual alphabet book

For Mary and Hebron

First published in Great Britain in 2014
by Amlap Publishing
PO Box 6144
Basildon
Essex SS14 0WX
www.amlappublishing.com

Acknowledgements
For their encouragement and support of her project to create this book, the author gives special thanks to Remi, Femi and Seun Sofowora, Mr and Mrs Onaolapo, Cath Bruzzone, Sam Hutchinson, Mrs Buki Ogunyemi, Mr Osho, Mrs Anna Forde, Ms Janet Sherlock, Ms Kate Brightmore, Mr Sunday Adogeri, Dekanla Jackson and Mr Sorungbe.

Special thanks go to Dr. Abba I. Tijani, University of Maiduguri, Nigeria, Dr. Sola Ajibade of Obafemi Awolowo University, Nigeria and Godson Bima for the translations, Ruth Nason for editorial help, Abiodun Dehinde for the illustrations and 432 Limited for the graphic design.

ISBN 978-0-9546116-4-4

Printed in Malaysia

amlap publishing

Aa

ENGLISH

apple

HAUSA

tuffa

IGBO

apụlụ

YORUBA

ápù OR ápùlù

Bb

ENGLISH

bicycle

HAUSA

keke

IGBO

anyịnya igwe

YORUBA

kẹ̀kẹ́

Cc

ENGLISH

chair

HAUSA

kujera

IGBO

oche

YORUBA

àga OR ìjókòó

Dd

ENGLISH

dog

HAUSA

kare

IGBO

nkịta

YORUBA

ajá

Ee

ENGLISH

egg

HAUSA

ƙwai

IGBO

akwa

YORUBA

eyin

Ff

ENGLISH

fingers

HAUSA

yatsu

IGBO

mkpịsịaka

YORUBA

Ìka ọwọ́

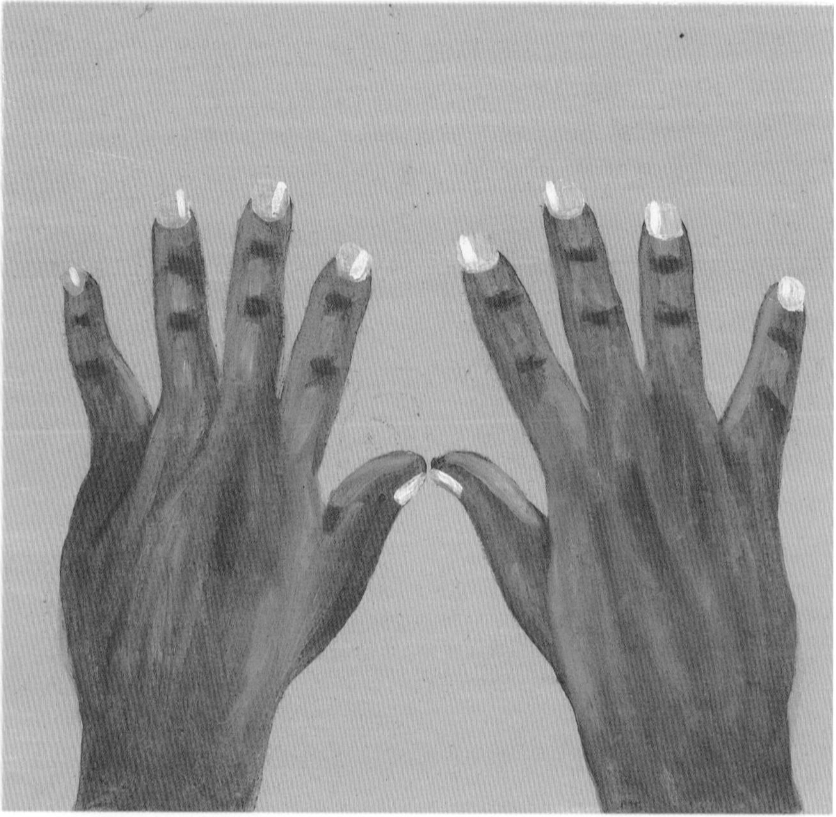

Gg

ENGLISH

glasses

HAUSA

tabarau

IGBO

ugegbe anya

YORUBA

ìgò OR awò ojú

Hh

ENGLISH

hen

HAUSA

kaza

IGBO

ọkụkọ

YORUBA

adìẹ

Ii

ENGLISH

ice cream

HAUSA

aiskirim

IGBO

ayịskrim

YORUBA

ice cream

Jj

ENGLISH

jug

HAUSA

tulu

IGBO

jọọgụ

YORUBA

ife

Kk

ENGLISH

key

HAUSA

makulli

IGBO

ọtụgha

YORUBA

kọ́kọ́rọ́

Ll

ENGLISH

lizard

HAUSA

ƙadangare

IGBO

ngwere

YORUBA

aláǹgba

Mm

ENGLISH

mosquito

HAUSA

sauro

IGBO

anwụnta

YORUBA

ẹ̀fọn OR yànmùyánmú

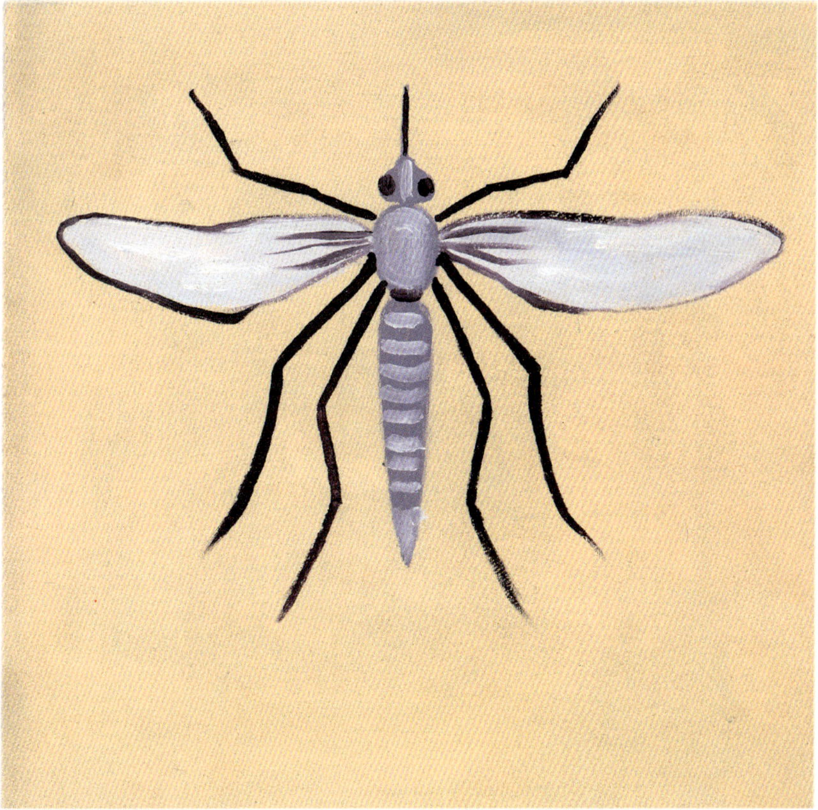

Nn

ENGLISH

necklace

HAUSA

abun wuya

IGBO

mgbaolu

YORUBA

ẹ̀gbà ọrùn

Oo

ENGLISH

ostrich

HAUSA

jumuna

IGBO

enyinnụnụ

YORUBA

ògòǹgò

Pp

ENGLISH

pencil

HAUSA

fensir

IGBO

mkpịsịakwụkwọ

YORUBA

pẹ́ńsùlù

Qq

ENGLISH

queen

HAUSA

sarauniya

IGBO

lọọlọ OR ugoeze

YORUBA

ayaba

Rr

ENGLISH

radio

HAUSA

rediyo

IGBO

redio

YORUBA

rédíò

Ss

ENGLISH

slippers

HAUSA

silifa

IGBO

slipas

YORUBA

sálúbàtà

Tt

ENGLISH

tree

HAUSA

maina

IGBO

osisi

YORUBA

igi

Uu

ENGLISH

umbrella

HAUSA

lema

IGBO

mbụlarị

YORUBA

òmbrélà OR agbòòrùn

Vv

ENGLISH

van

HAUSA

bilfodi

IGBO

ụgbọ van

YORUBA

bọ́ọ̀sì

Ww

ENGLISH

watch

HAUSA

agogo

IGBO

elekere

YORUBA

aago ọwọ́

Xx

ENGLISH

xylophone

HAUSA

molo

IGBO

ngelenge

YORUBA

sailofónù

Yy

ENGLISH

yam

HAUSA

doya

IGBO

ji

YORUBA

ịṣu

Zz

ENGLISH

zip

HAUSA

zif

IGBO

ziipu

YORUBA

síípù

ENGLISH

The English alphabet has 26 letters:

a b c d e f g h i j k l m n o p q r s t u v w x y z

A B C D E F G H I J K L M N O P Q R S T U V W X Y Z

HAUSA

There are 28 letters in the Hausa alphabet

a b ɓ c d ɗ e f g h i j k ƙ l m n o r s sh t ts u w y ƴ z

A B Ɓ C D Ɗ E F G H I J K Ƙ L M N O R S SH T TS U W Y Ƴ Z

IGBO

There are 36 letters in the Igbo alphabet:

a b ch d e f g gb gh gw h i ị j k kp kw l m n ñ nw ny o ọ p r s sh t u ụ v w y z

A B Ch D E F G Gb Gh Gw H I Ị J K Kp Kw L M N Ñ Nw Ny O Ọ P R S Sh T U Ụ V W Y Z

YORUBA

There are 25 letters in the Yoruba alphabet:

a b d e ẹ f g gb h i j k l m n o ọ p r s ṣ t u w y

A B D E Ẹ F G Gb H I J K L M N O Ọ P R S Ṣ T U W Y

Ijapa's Fun with the

o g

e n

g g

a n

i p

u g

Alphabet

apples

queen

umbrella

slippers

ice cream

mosquito

Ijapa's Fun with the Alphabet

Ijapa is trying to figure out the following puzzle. Can you help him?

you sit on one

you wear this around your neck

you use this to lock the door

Ijapa tells the time with it

Ijapa sees much better with these

This keeps you dry when it rains